Clinical Simulations for Teacher Development

A Companion Manual for Teachers

D1416921

Clinical Simulations for Teacher Development

A Companion Manual for Teachers

by

Benjamin H. Dotger
Syracuse University's School of Education

Information Age Publishing, Inc.
Charlotte, North Carolina • www.infoagepub.com

Library of Congress Cataloging-in-Publication Data

Dotger, Benjamin H.
Clinical simulations for teacher development : a companion manual for
teachers / by Benjamin H. Dotger.
pages cm
ISBN 978-1-62396-198-5 (paperback) -- ISBN 978-1-62396-199-2 (hardcover) --
ISBN 978-1-62396-200-5 (ebook) 1. Teachers--Training of. 2. Simulated
environment (Teaching method) I. Title.
LB1707.D68 2013
371.102--dc23

2012051101

Printed in the United States of America

CONTENTS

PREFACE

This companion manual is written to support teachers participating in clinical simulations. It is a step-by-step guide, providing all of the documentation teachers need prior to, during, and following their interactions with standardized individuals in a clinical learning environment. Clinical simulations are successful and most authentic when teacher participants operate *only* from this manual. To preserve the authenticity of a participant's experience in the simulations, this manual intentionally does not provide the other documentation and procedures required to successfully implement clinical simulations.

To fully implement the clinical simulations in this manual, teacher educators, teacher professional development coordinators, and/or education researchers should consult and operate from the more comprehensive, partner text, *"I Had No Idea": Clinical Simulations For Teacher Development.*

INTRODUCTION TO CLINICAL SIMULATIONS

As a novice high school English teacher, I had a lot to learn. Fortunately, I had solid mentors, good-natured students, and a stubborn streak that helped me learn from my mistakes. Looking back, I view my early years in the classroom as a series of very important experiences—collaborating with parents of students with special needs, supporting students who were exhausted from working three jobs, and navigating conversations with administrators whom I struggled to respect. These experiences—the tough conversations, the difficult explanations, and the unexpected questions and comments—often surprised me, but helped me become a more effective teacher.

This manual is designed to guide you through a series of clinical simulations that provide similar learning experiences. Unlike the readings or reflection papers that are common in teacher preparation programs, clinical simulations challenge you to enact what you know about teaching, instruction, and student support. We begin with an explanation of what a *simulation* actually involves, followed by an outline of the general procedures associated with simulations. This manual will *not* tell you what to expect from each simulation. That is intentional. Simulations are authentic only when you—as a teacher—engage in them using your own professional judgment and training. Providing you with a complete overview of each simulation in this manual—where you know ahead of time what questions you'll be asked and what challenges you'll encounter—would simply ruin the learning experience for you.

WHAT IS A CLINICAL SIMULATION?

In 1963, a neurologist at the University of Southern California by the name of Howard Barrows began utilizing standardized patients to enhance the preparation of future physicians (Barrows & Abrahamson, 1964). A standardized patient is a lay person, actor, or real patient who is carefully trained to present distinct symptoms and to communicate questions/concerns to medical professionals in training (e.g., preservice physicians, nurses, physical therapists) in a consistent, standard manner (Barrows, 1987, 1993, 2000). Thus, several standardized patients who are carefully trained to enact a particular medical case provide a common diagnostic and communication opportunity to large cohorts of future medical professionals. When large cohorts of future physicians, nurses, or physical therapists experience this common medical situation, the experience provides them and their medical education faculty opportunities for later analysis on potentially differing approaches to the same set of medical circumstances. Since its inception, medical education institutions have increasingly employed this simulated interaction pedagogy to prepare future medical professionals to accurately diagnose and communicate diagnoses/treatment regimens to patients. Although Barrows's idea was met with initial resistance, today over 95% of U.S. medical education institutions employ medical simulations to both teach and assess the clinical skills of future medical professionals (Coplan et al., 2008). Assessments of clinical diagnostic and interpersonal skills were incorporated into the U.S. Medical Licensing Examination in 2004 and medical education institution accreditation processes (Hauer et al., 2005; Islam & Zyphur, 2007).

FROM MEDICINE TO TEACHING:
CLINICAL SIMULATIONS FOR TEACHER DEVELOPMENT

As a teacher educator, I prepare future school professionals for their respective positions. In 2007, I was introduced to colleagues at SUNY Upstate Medical University, an institution geographically close to my own school of education. During our conversation, I learned about how SUNY Upstate uses standardized patients in clinical simulations to prepare its future doctors and physical therapists. After giving their work some thought, I returned a few days later, and asked these new colleagues if I could retrain some of their standardized patients to instead serve as standardized parents, standardized students, and standardized paraprofessionals. Beginning with that conversation, a wide variety of clinical simulations emerged, with the goal of providing teachers and school leaders with authentic learning experiences. Simply put, a clinical simulation is a live, face-to-face, interaction between a single teacher and a standardized individual (SI), where the teacher is presented with a variety of professional questions, challenges, and situations. In the next few pages, I will explain how you—as a teacher—will be expected to approach and navigate clinical simulations. To begin, I recount for you one of my challenges as first-year English teacher:

Chris Burton (pseudonym) was a student in my ninth grade English literature course. He never did anything terribly wrong, but was one of my most difficult students. Chris frequently interrupted me, talked nonstop with his peers near him, and typically stayed too long after class asking questions that had already been answered earlier in the class session. Chris's grades were not good. He never turned in his homework assignments and often appeared disorganized. Chris was a nice kid, but he seldom focused on the task at hand or grasped his role as a student. To Chris, school was an all-day social event where he utilized his big smile and excessive energy.

After approximately one-third of the semester had passed, I was thoroughly frustrated with Chris and wrote to his mother, Jenny, asking her if she could come in for a parent-teacher conference. This was to be my first parent-teacher conference, but I didn't prepare for it. I knew that I needed Chris to "do better", but when Jenny Burton walked into my classroom for our conference, I had no idea what to say or how to say it.

For 20 minutes that afternoon, I struggled to convey to Ms. Burton why I had requested a conference with her. I kept saying Chris was a "nice kid," but that was about as concrete as I could be. Because I didn't prepare, I struggled to give specific examples that illustrated my broader concerns for Chris. When she asked me questions and made specific statements about Chris, I failed to address her perspectives and ideas. It was not my best professional moment, and I imagine Ms. Burton left our conference wondering why I'd taken up her valuable time.

THE PERSON SITTING ACROSS THE TABLE: STANDARDIZED INDIVIDUALS (SIs)

You, too, will have an opportunity to speak with Jenny Burton. The Jenny Burton you meet, though, will be a SI, an actor carefully trained to portray Ms. Burton. In the *Burton* simulation, you and your peers will sit down one-to-one, face-to-face, with Jenny Burton in a conference room. Your responsibility is to speak with Ms. Burton about Chris, who is a student in your classroom. As you interact with Ms. Burton, she is trained to present to you specific professional questions and contexts. This simulation, like the others represented in this manual, was carefully crafted to provide you opportunities to practice navigating and refining your professional knowledge, skills, and dispositions.

Every simulation supported by this manual presents you with a different SI with whom you will interact. If facilitated properly, you will not know or recognize the SIs you meet in simulations. This is intentional. Simulations are *not* role-plays, where you and a peer act out a specific concept, with "wink and nod" grins on your faces. Instead, simulations are designed to situate you in very realistic professional environments, where you encounter teaching 'problems of practice' for which you could not reasonably predict or prepare. The authenticity of the simulated environment is preserved only when the situation very closely mirrors daily teaching practices. Authenticity dissolves, however, if you are placed in front of an SI that you know, recognize, or are any way affiliated.

HOW DO I KNOW WHAT'S GOING ON?:
TEACHER INTERACTION PROTOCOLS

This simulation manual provides you with twelve Teacher Interaction Protocols. Each protocol supports a different simulation, providing you—as the teacher—with all *reasonable and appropriate* information you need to know in order to engage in the simulation. I intentionally highlight the phrase *reasonable and appropriate*. Some simulations—like *Jenny Burton*—situate you in a conference that you initiated. As the teacher who has initiated a conference with a parent, you would have an appropriate reason for doing so and you would have a general understanding of the contexts and issues supporting your request for a conference. Thus, the Teacher Interaction Protocol that supports the *Jenny Burton* simulation gives you plenty of information on Chris, his mannerisms, characteristics, and actions that are causing you concern. As you get ready to step into conference with Jenny Burton, you know (from the Teacher Interaction Protocol) what led you to have this conversation. How you choose to approach and navigate the conversation, however, is entirely up to you and is not dictated by the Teacher Interaction Protocol.

In contrast, some simulations are not initiated by you (the teacher) and are instead initiated by the (standardized) parent, colleague, or student. In these situations, your Teacher Interaction Protocol will provide only limited information, and will not indicate the purpose of the conference. You will find yourself entering into these clinical simulations without knowing what to expect from the parent, student, or colleague. Although it may feel unreasonable, this type of learning experience is intentionally designed to mirror the reality of spur-of-the-moment professional interactions that occur when parents, students, or colleagues raise questions, express concerns, or make statements that teachers did not anticipate or initiate. Ultimately, as professional educators, we often find ourselves in conversations with parents, student, and colleagues that we could not predict, cannot control, but still must engage thoughtfully.

The Teacher Interaction Protocols describe schools, classrooms, students, colleagues, and communities that may or may not resemble those with which you are familiar. Occasionally, a teacher participant will read a protocol and say, "This doesn't sound like the classrooms I've observed or worked in." As you can imagine, it is impossible to construct simulated environments that mirror the exact circumstances in which every teacher has trained or worked. To do so is impractical, and it defeats the purpose of constructing a "shared learning experience" where all teachers engage with the same simulated challenges and contexts. While Teacher Interaction Protocols cannot be tailored to individual teachers to a finite degree, all protocols situate you, as the teacher, in the position of a proactive and ethical educator. These simulations are *not* designed to place you in a deficit position from the very start. For example, no Teacher Interaction Protocol will ever indicate that you called a student "stupid" and then situate you in front of that student's very angry parents who demand explanation. Placing you in such a deficit position before you ever step into the simulation room makes it easy for you—as the teacher—to disregard any authenticity to the simulation by simply stating, "I wouldn't say that to a student in real life." While you start each simulation from a neutral position, it is important to remember that you are accountable as the teacher throughout the simulation. Thus, if you make an unethical statement, a questionable decision, or a poor assumption during the simulation, you should expect the SI to respond in accordance with his/her training.

Most importantly, Teacher Interaction Protocols provide you background and contextual information, but *in no way shape, direct, or script your actions, decisions, or verbalizations* in the simulations. The SI has very specific questions, comments, and statements to convey to you in a simulation, but what you say, do, and decide is entirely up to you.

WHO ARE WE TALKING ABOUT?: THE HYPOTHETICAL STUDENT

In medical simulations, future doctors, nurses, and physical therapists engage with standardized patients, live persons who present distinct symptoms to the professionals for diagnosis and treatment. On occasion, though, certain medical simulations call for the use of a hypothetical person. For example, consider an encounter between a future nurse and a standardized patient who presents clear signs of physical and emotional abuse. During a typical in-take conversation, the nurse will gather data from the standardized patient on the domestic incident that led to the hospital visit. A well-trained standardized patient—operating from a standardized patient protocol—will articulate the events surrounding the abuse. When asked, the standardized patient will describe the abuser and the specific incident. If asked additional questions about her general well being, safety, and others (e.g., children) that might be subject to similar abuse, the standardized patient is also able to give a very detailed response about people and household contexts that do not actually exist. That is, the standardized patient describes her hypothetical son and daughter, who are also residing in this abusive household. While the standardized patient is physically present in front of the nurse, everything and everyone else described by the standardized patient is hypothetical.

Most of the clinical simulations supported by this manual focus on teacher-parent interactions. As the teacher, you will engage with a SI portraying a parent. While the standardized parent is live and sitting across the table from you, your conversation will still focus on a hypothetical student. For clarity on how hypothetical students are incorporated into a conversation between a teacher and standardized parent, consider again the *Burton* simulation.

Jenny Burton is a recently divorced single mother with a teenage son, Chris. The Teacher Interaction Protocol for the *Burton* simulation describes who Chris is, his general demeanor in your class, his academic and behavioral performances, and the steps you have taken to encourage Chris to make improvements. As you read the protocol, use the descriptive information in it to help you envision the hypothetical "Chris." Through your prior field experiences in classrooms, you've probably already met students similar to those described in the protocols. Prior to the *Burton* simulation, you need to envision a "Chris," use the information provided in the protocol, and conduct the conference with Jenny Burton using your best professional judgment. Because the *Burton* simulation tends to be one's first simulation experience, teachers sometimes indicate they are unsure about a discussion with a standardized parent, in which they are talking about a hypothetical student who does not actually exist. After their first simulation, though, teacher participants indicate they could actually function in the simulation by relying closely on the data in the protocol and by preparing themselves, beforehand, with a mental image of the hypothetical student.

PRE-/POSTSIMULATION REFLECTION QUESTIONS

For each simulation in this manual, you'll find a Teacher Interaction Protocol, followed by pre- and postsimulation questions. As suggested by its prefix, you should answer the pre-simulation reflection questions *before* you enter the simulation room. These questions are designed to elicit from you any plans of action, professional approaches, questions/concerns, and dialogue you anticipate or intend to implement when the simulation begins. Your interpretation of the Teacher Interaction Protocol, along with your own professional training, will guide your responses to the presimulation questions.

The postsimulation questions are more extensive than the pre-simulation questions. I encourage you to answer the postsimulation questions very soon *after* you conclude your clinical simulation. I ask my own teacher participants to respond to these questions within 20 minutes of the conclusion of their simulations. You should ask your simulation facilitator whether s/he wants you to review your simulation video *before or after* you respond to the post-simulation questions. Reviewing your video is a very important part of the reflection process. Accessing your video *before* you construct responses to the post-simulation questions will give you a broader, (video) data-informed perspective on your simulation. Reviewing your video *after* you have constructed responses to the post-simulation questions allows you to compare your initial postsimulation perspective with the broader perspective that the full video account will later offer.

Importantly, the post-simulation questions do not explicitly reference the SI's questions, concerns, and/or statements that you would have just experienced in the recently-concluded simulation. This is intentional. Making reference to the SI's dialogue in the postsimulation questions risks divulging the content of the simulation itself; all one would have to do before a simulation is look at the postsimulation questions to determine what challenges are included in the simulation. The goal of any simulation is to provide you with an authentic opportunity to engage in a variety of professional challenges that emerge through service in schools. In your daily practices within schools, you do not have an opportunity to preview the questions or concerns that parents or students will express to you. Instead, you are challenged to address them in the moment. To preserve this "in-the-moment" challenge, the SI's questions, concerns, and statements are not listed or alluded to in any of your documents in this manual, including the postsimulation reflection questions. Only your simulation facilitator has the training protocols for the SIs you will meet in the simulations.

FREQUENTLY ASKED QUESTIONS

There are a few common questions that teachers ask before, during, or after their clinical simulations. Responses (below) to the most frequent inquiries provide you with clarification and a broader understanding of the clinical simulation experience:

1.   How should I do this?: "Use your best professional judgment"

Each simulation is an approximation of practice, where a teacher can practice enacting professional knowledge, skills, and dispositions, and later review and reflect on what s/he said and did in simulation. To that end, there is no one "right" or "correct" way to navigate any given simulation.

Before a simulation, if you were to ask me, "How should I do this?," I would reply, "Use your best professional judgment, knowledge, and skills!" This is the only guidance and direction that I give teachers before a simulation, beyond providing them with the information in the Teacher Interaction Protocol. Sometimes, teacher participants are frustrated by my unwillingness to tell them 'how' to approach a simulation. My rationale is this—clinical simulations represent opportunities for the synthesis and application of professional knowledge and skills acquired through earlier teacher preparation coursework. Taking what one knows as a professional and applying it in a (simulated) environment suggests that the teacher will make decisions and engage in actions that s/he believes to be just, correct, and appropriate. I *do not* want teachers to engage in a simulation according to a step-by-step plan that I outlined for them beforehand on how to address an upset parent. Similarly, I *do not* want teachers to simply mimic what I told them to say to a struggling student. Ultimately, I want teachers to take ownership of their professional actions, decisions, and articulations.

Remember, clinical simulations represent opportunities to practice and reflect. During a simulation, enact your own professional judgment and skills, not the approaches that you think others want to see or hear.

2.   What if I mess up?: "There is no pause button"

When I provide orientation to teachers preparing for simulations, I emphasize that the SI will never break character. For example, if a teacher asks to "start (the simulation) over" or says to the standardized parent, "Oh, I goofed up! Can I try that again?", the SI will respond in character by saying, "What do you mean by 'start over'? I don't understand what's going on; I thought we were talking about my (son/daughter)!" In essence, the SI will always remain in character and will never acknowledge any circumstance(s) or request(s) outside of the simulated environment.

Not all conversations or decisions unfold smoothly or as anticipated. No teacher is perfect, in simulation or in daily practice. If you believe you have made a mistake in your interactions with the SI, then use your professional judgment and skills to remedy that mistake as effectively as possible.

3. Who is watching my simulation?

The basic answer to this question is, "No one other than you." Simulations are fast, demanding, visceral experiences. As a result, it is often difficult for teachers to recall with clarity the significant dialogue, decision-making, and response patterns that unfolded in the simulation. Simulations are video-recorded to provide you—the teacher participant—with a clear account of exactly what was said and what decisions were made when you met with the SI.

A preservice teacher once reported to me that she watched her first simulation video as she hid in her dorm room closet. Laughing sheepishly, she recounted how she sat there, petrified of what her roommates would think if they walked in her room and saw her *Jenny Burton* simulation video. Later that very evening, though, this preservice teacher articulated and reflected on an impressive number of decisions, assumptions, and considerations she made when speaking with Jenny Burton. Despite her fear of having someone else see her simulation performance, she drew heavily from the video data to inform her verbal and written post-simulation reflections.

You may be asked by your simulation facilitator to present segments of your simulation video to your peers, who also engaged in the same simulation. This is a very valuable opportunity, where you can all view each other's approaches to the same professional challenges that the SI presented to each of you. Quite commonly, sharing your simulation experiences with others who faced the same circumstances builds a strong professional learning community. That said, you do not have to share your video. It is for your professional learning only. Note that any person asking to review or use your video for research purposes must present to you a consent form for your signature.

4. How long should my simulation last?

You have a maximum of 22 minutes of time in each simulation. At the 20-minute mark, your simulation facilitator will knock on the simulation room door, gently interrupt your dialogue, and indicate that you have "an upcoming meeting." This is your cue to conclude the simulation. DO NOT simply leave the simulation room as soon as this time cue is given. Instead, appropriately conclude your simulation with the SI within the next couple of minutes.

Although you have a maximum of 22 minutes, you do not have to "fill" that time. If you engage in a simulation, and you feel that it has come to an appropriate resolution in 11 minutes, then conclude it and exit the simulation room. Do not feel like you have to make conversation or stall in a simulation in order to reach a certain time mark. Within reason, there is no requirement or expectation that a simulation last a minimum amount of time. Obviously, if you're in a simulation with a struggling (standardized) student, and you spend only 1½ minutes with that student, then your simulation facilitator might reasonably suggest you could have spent more time supporting that student.

5. Why are we doing this?

This is a question that I do not normally receive from teachers. However, this is a question that I often address in professional essays and journal articles. Many teacher education programs rely on traditional methods for preparing teachers to engage in increasingly challenging public school contexts. As teacher prep programs continue to use stagnant college course structures, the classroom environments that teachers are preparing for continue to rapidly evolve. This classic gap between teacher education and teacher practice will continue to grow until the methodologies by which teachers are prepared more closely align with the challenges presented in classrooms.

Essentially, clinical simulations can better prepare novice teachers for the realities of serving in public schools. Simply asking my preservice teachers to read a chapter about working with parents and write a reflection allows them to completely disconnect from the importance of the topic. By the time preservice teachers are in my college courses, they are quite adept at writing the bland, jargon-filled reflections they believe I want to read, but which actually reflect that they have little or no practical experience from which to draw. When I challenge my preservice teachers, though, to engage with the concerned parent sitting across the table, and to write a reflection based on the resulting video data, I do not allow them to disengage from the importance, immediacy, and value of the topic.

So, why are we doing this? For the experience! The clinical environment allows teacher educators to provide preservice teachers with a very broad range of experiences often not available through field placements in schools. The use of SIs allows teacher educators to provide many preservice teachers with a common, shared experience, on which individual and whole group learning is based. Simulations serve as formative learning experiences, helping novice teachers formulate, "try-on" and practice their emerging identities as "teachers." Simulations are also forgiving, though. They are not summative evaluations or high-stakes, single encounters in public schools, where the consequences of poor decision-making can be quite significant. To engage in clinical simulations means that novice teachers learn from authentic practice.

REFERENCES

Barrows, H. S. (1987). *Simulated (standardized) patients and other human simulations: A comprehensive guide to their training and use in teaching and evaluation.* Chapel Hill, NC: Health Sciences Consortium.

Barrows, H. S. (1993). An overview of the uses of standardized patients for teaching and evaluating clinical skills. *Academic Medicine, 68*(6), 443-453.

Barrows, H. S. (2000). *Problem-based learning applied to medical education.* Springfield, IL: Southern Illinois University Press.

Barrows, H. S., & Abrahmson, S. (1964). The programmed patient: A technique for appraising student performance in clinical neurology. *Journal of Medical Education, 39*, 802-805.

Coplan, B., Essary, A. C., Lohenry, K., & Stoehr, J. D. (2008). An update on the utilization of standardized patients in physician assistant education. *The Journal of Physician Assistant Education, 19*(4), 14-19.

Hauer, K. E., Hodgson, C. S., Kerr, K. M., Teherani, A., & Irby, D. M. (2005). A national study of medical student clinical skills assessment. *Academic Medicine, 80*(10), S25-S29.

Islam, G., & Zyphur, M. (2007). Ways of interacting: The standardization of communication in medical training. *Human Relations, 60*(5), 769-792.

HOW TO USE THE COMPANION MANUAL

The remainder of this manual provides you with the documents necessary to engage in 12 different clinical simulations. Three documents support each simulation—a Teacher Interaction Protocol, a presimulation teacher reflection guide, and a postsimulation teacher reflection guide. These documents provide you with space to record your observations, notes, and written reflections.

A simulation facilitator will guide you through the clinical simulations outlined in this manual. Your facilitator will provide you with the name, order, and logistics of the simulations in which you will engage and for which you should prepare. Typically, teacher participants have 5 to 7 days notice prior to engaging in a clinical simulation. In preparation, carefully read the appropriate Teacher Interaction Protocol, making notes on this document as needed. You may keep this protocol with you during the simulation if you prefer. After reviewing the protocol, respond to the prompts in the Presimulation Teacher Reflection Guide. Your responses to these prompts document your goals, questions, anticipations, and strategies prior to your participation in the actual simulation.

In each clinical simulation, you will engage with a standardized individual (e.g., a standardized student, parent, or paraprofessional). Following your simulation, respond to the prompts in the Postsimulation Teacher Reflection Guide. Each clinical simulation is videorecorded for your professional reflection. Note that your simulation facilitator will indicate whether or not you should use your simulation video recording to inform your responses on the postsimulation prompts.

Clinical Simulations for Teacher Development: A Companion Manual for Teachers, pp. 1–47

1

Jenny Burton Simulation

TEACHER INTERACTION PROTOCOL

STUDENT:	CHRIS BURTON Male, Age 14, Lower SES, 9th Grade, GPA: N/A
CONFERENCE TYPE:	Teacher-initiated

Chris Burton is one of 26 students in your 9th grade _____ class. During the first 10 days of the new semester, you have assigned and collected four classroom assignments, three of which Chris did not turn in at all. Chris did submit the first assignment, having completed only two-thirds of the requirements, and received a "70" as the first grade of his high school career.

At times, Chris appears to be daydreaming. During your minilectures, in-class assignments, and small group exercises, he is often looking around the classroom. His attention appears to be focused on classroom objects (posters, displays, etc.) and his peers, but not on the current subject at hand or any students that are actively participating in classroom discussions or activities. When you call on Chris to answer a question or to ask his opinion, he snaps to attention and appears a bit sheepish. You've noticed that unless you call his name first and then ask him a question, he is lost and does not actively recall what was happening in the classroom.

In addition to Chris's tendency to daydream, you've noticed that he resists being "on-task" and is eager to speak with the two students that sit to his right (one female, one male). Typically, his resistance to classwork occurs within the first ten minutes of the 1-hour class session. You've noticed that once you get Chris focused, something you've been able to do only by staying in close proximity to him, he is usually on-task with his classwork for about 20 minutes. By the second half of class, Chris is usually drifting off and no longer paying attention.

You've spoken with Chris on two occasions with regard to his grades (one "70" and three zeros). During these interactions, Chris is always polite, and appears sincere when promising to submit future work on time. You've spoken with Chris on seven different occasions with regard to his daydreaming and chattiness. Five of these "chats" were gentle reminders to pay attention, be quiet, and/or to stay focused. On two occasions, you spoke with Chris after the final bell rang, reminding him to stay focused on his classwork and to refrain from talking to his peers. When you speak to him, Chris is always polite and is occasionally apologetic for not "doing better."

The first 10 days with Chris have presented both academic and behavioral challenges. You consult with the school's counselor, learning that Chris is off to a rough academic start in all of his classes. For these reasons, you've decided to contact Chris's mother and request a conference. She is the only parent listed on Chris's "Student Info" card. When you spoke with Ms. Burton by phone to request the parent conference, she sounded a bit surprised. You explained that you had some concerns about Chris's progress so far in the semester and wanted to speak with her personally to address any academic or behavioral difficulties before they became more serious issues. Ms. Burton agreed, thanked you, and was willing to rearrange her work schedule to meet with you immediately after school.

Presimulation Teacher Reflection Guide —*Jenny Burton*

1. Based on the description of Chris Burton in the Teacher Interaction Protocol, what do you anticipate during this conference with his mother, Jenny?

2. As Chris's teacher, you initiated this conference with his mother. Considering Chris's performance and behavior in your classroom, what goals do you have for this upcoming conference?

3. Do you have any specific observations, notes, or statements you wish to document before this clinical simulation begins?

4. Do you have any questions, concerns, or professional issues that you wish to document before this clinical simulation begins?

Postsimulation Teacher Reflection Guide —*Jenny Burton*

1. Reflecting back on your conversation with Jenny Burton, what are your initial thoughts and feelings?

2. Did the conference with Jenny Burton occur as you had anticipated?

3. Were you able to accomplish your goals? If not, what prevented you from doing so?

4. What were your strengths in this clinical simulation? Briefly describe the portion of the simulation where you exhibited this professional strength.

5. Did this clinical simulation highlight any professional skills, knowledge base(s), or dispositions on which you need to improve? If so, briefly describe the specific portion of the simulation where you struggled or were unsure of how to proceed.

6. As you reflect on the entire *Jenny Burton* simulation, do you have any new or different perspectives on your professional roles or responsibilities?

7. Are there specific questions, statements, dilemmas, or situations that arose in your clinical simulation that you want to raise for discussion during the larger group debriefing process? (List below. If possible, include a time signature from the video recording of your simulation.

Donald Bolden Simulation

TEACHER INTERACTION PROTOCOL

STUDENT: LAURA BOLDEN
                                    Female, Upper Middle Class SES, 10th
                                    Grade Age: 15, GPA 4.0

CONFERENCE TYPE: Parent-initiated

Laura Bolden is a student in your 10th grade honors (Insert Subject) class. She has consistently demonstrated a command of the subject matter in your class and in her other classes. The variety of classroom assignments has given you a chance to review Laura's excellent writing, as she is articulate, concise, and captivating in written expression. You've complimented her in the past, noting for her that she is quite advanced in this skill beyond even the AP 12 grade (Insert Subject) requirements. Although generally a quiet person, she does interact daily with three other students in your class, often going to lunch with one of them. Laura does not say much in class, but when she does offer her opinion or answer a question, her responses are always thoughtful.

Laura's academic abilities are not what distinguish her for most people that she comes in contact with on a daily basis. Laura is significantly obese. During her two semesters in high school, the guidance department has carefully and appropriately spoken with her teachers, arranging a special seat and desk to accommodate Laura. At the beginning of this semester (her 10th grade year), you provided this accommodation for Laura within a cluster of 12 desks for this small honors class.

One important assignment in your class involves a public speaking exercise, where students choose a topic that is important to them and present a formal 3-5 minute speech on that subject. Impressively, Laura chose to speak on the challenges of obesity and her experiences in working to improve her health. Her speech was excellent in both content and delivery. Recognizing the connection between Laura's topic and her physical presence, her peers were very respectful and receptive during her speech. She smiled as she completed her speech and you remember thinking that although this was a small, relatively-safe honors class, her presentation of that topic took real guts, particularly for a 10th grader.

In the spring of Laura's sophomore year, you noticed that she appeared more anxious and nervous than in the past. On the Monday following the weekend of the spring formal, you observed an upset Laura who constantly looked down at her desk with puffy eyes and flushed cheeks. Laura remained quite sad, and 3 weeks after the spring formal she delivered to you a sealed envelope. The envelope contained a respect-fully written but brief letter from her father, requesting a conference with you at your earliest convenience. Your initial phone call was immediately returned, and you arranged a conference with her father after school for later that week.

Presimulation Teacher Reflection Guide —*Donald Bolden*

1. Based on the more extensive description of Laura Bolden in the Teacher Interaction Protocol, what do you anticipate during this conference with her father, Donald?

2. As Laura's teacher, you know her to be a productive student. Considering Laura's performance in your classroom and the fact that Mr. Bolden initiated this conference, what goals do you have?

3. Do you have any specific observations, notes, or statements you wish to document before this clinical simulation begins?

4. Do you have any questions, concerns, or professional issues that you wish to document before this clinical simulation begins?

Postsimulation Teacher Reflection Guide —*Donald Bolden*

1. Reflecting back on your conversation with Donald Bolden, what are your initial thoughts and feelings?

2. Did the conference with Mr. Bolden occur as you had anticipated?

3. Were you able to accomplish your goals? If not, what prevented you from doing so?

4. What were your strengths in this clinical simulation? Briefly describe the portion of the simulation where you exhibited this professional strength.

5. Did this clinical simulation highlight any professional skills, knowledge base(s), or dispositions on which you need to improve? If so, briefly describe the specific portion of the simulation where you struggled or were unsure of how to proceed.

6. Consider the nonacademic aspects of this clinical simulation. As you reflect on the *Donald Bolden* simulation, do you have any new or different perspectives on your professional roles or responsibilities?

7. Are there specific questions, statements, dilemmas, or situations
   · that arose in your clinical simulation that you want to raise for discussion during the larger group debriefing process? (List below. If possible, include a time signature from the video recording of your simulation.)

Jennifer Turner Simulation

TEACHER INTERACTION PROTOCOL

STUDENT: AMBER TURNER
                           Female, Affluent, GPA: 2.4, 11th Grade
CONFERENCE TYPE: Parent-initiated

Pleasantville High School is located in the town of Pleasantville, VA, a small, rural, bedroom community 1 hour away from a large, congested, metropolitan city. People who live in Pleasantville work in occupations that require commuting to the large city or that are based on agriculture. Consequently, the community maintains an overall lower middle class socioeconomic status. While the community consists of "a little bit of everyone," its population is predominantly Caucasian, conservative, and traditional.

You are beginning the second semester of your first year of teaching at Pleasantville HS, having taught SAT prep, peer helper, and freshman seminar courses in addition to your primary (Insert Subject Area) courses. In your first year as a teacher, you've become an integral part of the faculty, assuming sponsorship responsibilities for various clubs, lending your time and support to numerous after-school events and activities (prom, athletics, talent shows, etc.), and serving on the principal's advisory council. You've established an overall solid rapport with your students, as they recognize you as a teacher who is fair, consistent, knowledgeable, and has high expectations for student achievement. In general, you are exhausted by your various responsibilities and at times you question if you've taken on too much and can perform well in all your various roles.

One of your courses is a general (Insert Subject Area) course for 11th grade students. Many of the students in this class have aspirations for blue-collar careers, citing the successes of family members who didn't go to college and "have done just fine." Those students who do show interest in attending college often have aspirations that are not congruent with their actual grades; that is, they want to be doctors and lawyers, but they maintain C-/D+ GPAs. In general, this particular group of students is quite personable, but seems to always be testing your limits and expectations. You've found that discipline policies must be enforced much more often and you constantly encourage them to get these students to be minimally productive.

As a teacher, you believe that all students can learn. You structure your classes such that you support students as they grow intellectually while always keeping the academic pressure on, challenging them to continue advancing and to not become passive, stagnant individuals who just show up for class. This philosophy translates to a variety of independent in-class and out-of-class assignments. Never a fan of long lectures or worksheets, you structure most classes with a combination of minilectures, independent and group readings, and in-class projects/assignments. At times, students show frustration with the variety of learning activities. Some students appear to be more comfortable with you simply telling them what they will need to know, instead of challenging them to discover and construct knowledge themselves. One of your greatest challenges is fostering a scholarly environment with this group of students, as many struggle with the relevance of (Insert Your Subject) , and how it can possibly impact their futures.

Amber Turner is a student in this class, but has made it clear that academics are not her focus. She is known throughout the small Pleasantville community as "the model," having appeared in several well-known clothing store and shoe commercials/photo shoots. Amber displays unmistakable arrogance and disdain for her peers and teachers. A quick temper and a sarcastic tongue compliment her personality, and she is always quite nasty in what she has to say to anyone she doesn't like. In the initial weeks that Amber has been in your course, your upbeat tone and clear command of the classroom have fended off any direct confrontation with Amber, although you note that she seems to always be muttering under her breath with her like-minded friends.

It is clear to you that Amber sees high school as a waste of her time, as she is solely focused on her modeling career. The school's guidance counselor reports to you that she is maintaining a healthy "C" average in her other classes. In your class, though, her grades are in the low "60s," resulting from a variety of absences and incomplete work. When she is in attendance and completes her work, her grades are sufficient—not the best completed assignments you've ever seen, but not "F" quality either. Amber's facial expressions, vocal sighs, and rolling eyes tell you she'd prefer a class where she didn't have to work, and where you just gave her the info and she regurgitated it back to you on a test. Your constructivist approach to (Insert Subject), though, causes Amber and her peers to actually have to put forth some effort.

You know that Amber is frustrated, and you're not surprised when you receive a somewhat curt handwritten note from her mother, requesting a conference with you. The note provides a list of days and times that her mother is available, and in light of expediting the conference, you inform Amber of a day/time that best suits your schedule, telling Amber that you're happy to meet her mother at the school. In response, Amber gives you a smirk and a distinct "now you're going to catch hell" look.

Presimulation Teacher Reflection Guide —*Jennifer Turner*

1. Based on the Teacher Interaction Protocol, what do you anticipate during this conference with Amber's mother, Jennifer? Are there specific parts of the protocol that stand out to you?

2. As Amber's teacher, you have faced some challenges to policies and procedures. In preparation for your conference with her mother, Jennifer, what goals do you have?

3. Do you have any specific observations, notes, or statements you wish to document before this clinical simulation begins?

4. Do you have any questions, concerns, or professional issues that you wish to document before this clinical simulation begins?

Postsimulation Teacher Reflection Guide —*Jennifer Turner*

1. Reflecting back on your conversation with Jennifer Turner, what are your initial thoughts and feelings?

2. Did the conference with Mrs. Turner occur as you had anticipated?

3. Were you able to accomplish your goals? If not, what prevented you from doing so?

4. What were your strengths in this clinical simulation? Briefly describe the portion of the simulation where you exhibited this professional strength.

5. Did this clinical simulation highlight any professional skills, knowledge base(s), or dispositions on which you need to improve? If so, briefly describe the specific portion of the simulation where you struggled or were unsure of how to proceed.

6. This clinical simulation addressed issues related to classroom policies and teacher expectations. Reflecting on your meeting with Mrs. Turner, do you have any new or different perspectives on your professional responsibilities, policies, or expectations?

7. Are there specific questions, statements, dilemmas, or situations that arose in your clinical simulation that you want to raise for discussion during the larger group debriefing process? (List below. If possible, include a time signature from the video recording of your simulation.)

Jim Smithers Simulation

TEACHER INTERACTION PROTOCOL

STUDENT: ALLISON SMITHERS
                            Female, Affluent, 10th grade, GPA 4.2
                            (A+)
CONFERENCE TYPE: Parent-initiated

Note: This clinical simulation focuses on a reading assignment in association with a school-wide, extracurricular reading initiative. It is designed to be applicable to teacher participants in any subject area, not just English/language arts.

You are the teacher for a 10th grade honors (Insert Subject), a course intentionally designed to challenge students as they actively prepare themselves for various 4-year colleges. While your class is not technically listed as an "AP" (advanced placement) course, you advertise and teach it as such, requiring extensive work on the part of the students both in and outside of the classroom. Although you are a novice teacher, your course has become well known and respected among honors students for its intellectual demand and rigor.

Allison Smithers is a student in this class. Although generally more quiet than the rest of her peers, she has proven herself to be very thoughtful, considerate, and one of the most academically gifted individuals in this group of 24 students. Her comments and contributions are always incredibly additive to the subject at hand, and you've come to rely on her as a key individual in your classroom. Through her contributions during classroom discussions and in her written assignments, you've learned that Allison's future plans involve enrolling in nursing school, and then using that training in a desired Peace Corp position.

During the second semester of this year-long course, you receive a hand-written note from Allison's father, delivered very sheepishly by Allison at the end of class one Friday afternoon. He is requesting a conference with you "as soon as possible," indicating that he is "very concerned" about one of the assignments you've given Allison and her peers. After reading this note, you ask Allison for more information. Continuing to look embarrassed and afraid, she says "I'm uncomfortable with the assigned reading, *Siddhartha*."

You call Mr. Smithers that afternoon and arrange to meet with him Monday afternoon in your classroom. Mr. Smithers is polite, but curt, as the conversation to arrange the conference is very short and doesn't give you any additional information with regard to his concerns. Thus, you spend most of the weekend pondering the additional reading you've assigned to Allison and her peers. You assigned this reading as part of the larger school-wide initiative that requires each teacher (regardless of the subject matter s/he teaches) to select a book from the school's approved reading list and to assign it to their classes for extracurricular reading emphasis. The reading you chose from the list is *Siddhartha*, a novel about a young Buddhist man on a life quest, searching for his role in the world and how to make meaning from his existence. At one point in the novel, the author, Herman Hess, references the main character, Siddhartha, and his interaction with a prostitute. The word "breast" is used in *brief* reference to the prostitute that Siddhartha encounters.

Presimulation Teacher Reflection Guide —*Jim Smithers*

1. Based on the Teacher Interaction Protocol, what do you anticipate during this conference with Allison's father, Jim? Are there specific parts of the protocol that stand out to you?

2. In association with a school-wide reading initiative, you have assigned Allison and her peers the novel, *Siddhartha*. What goals do you have for your meeting with Mr. Smithers?

3. Do you have any specific observations, notes, or statements you wish to document before this clinical simulation begins?

4. Do you have any questions, concerns, or professional issues that you wish to document before this clinical simulation begins?

Postsimulation Teacher Reflection Guide —*Jim Smithers*

Note: This clinical simulation focuses on a reading assignment in association with a school-wide, extracurricular reading initiative. It is designed to be applicable to teacher participants in any subject area, not just English/language arts.

1. Reflecting on your conversation with Mr. Smithers, what are your initial thoughts and feelings?

2. Did the conference with Jim Smithers occur as you had anticipated?

3. Were you able to accomplish your goals? If not, what prevented you from doing so?

4. What were your strengths in this clinical simulation? Briefly describe the portion of the simulation where you exhibited this professional strength.

5. Did this clinical simulation highlight any professional skills, knowledge base(s), or dispositions on which you need to improve? If so, briefly describe the specific portion of the simulation where you struggled or were unsure of how to proceed.

6. Reflecting on your meeting with Mr. Smithers, do you have any new or different perspectives on your professional responsibilities, policies, or expectations? Additionally, did this simulation result in new perspectives on school or school district policies?

7. Are there specific questions, statements, dilemmas, or situations that arose in your clinical simulation that you want to raise for discussion during the larger group debriefing process? (List below. If possible, include a time signature from the video recording of your simulation.)

Angela Summers Simulation

TEACHER INTERACTION PROTOCOL

STUDENT: DAVID SUMMERS
                      Male, Middle Class SES, GPA: 1.4
CONFERENCE TYPE: Teacher-initiated

David Summers is a student in your 11th grade regular (Insert Subject) course. His current average in your course is a 28. This performance is a result of very poor test grades, failure to submit any completed assignments, and constant attendance and behavioral issues. Essentially, he just sits there, making it clear through his body language and actions that he will not be doing any of the work you've requested. He laughs and talks with his friends, but smirks and ignores any adult figure. He and his girlfriend are often kissing in a nearby stairwell during lunch periods. David is loud in the hallways, uses profanity openly, and seems to have a complete disregard for anyone around him. At the midpoint of the fall semester, you requested a parent conference via phone call and written letter. You received no reply from either his mother or stepfather.

In addition to repeated written and verbal attempts to contact David's parents at home, you've spent quite a bit of time reprimanding, conferencing, and disciplining him before, during and after class. Recognizing early a pattern of problems, you've thoroughly documented every issue with David in your class file. Nothing seems to be working. In fact, at the 14-week mark in the semester, David is in an academic and behavioral tailspin. In particular, David demonstrated his complete disregard for his peers and for teachers during an event that happened last Friday.

On this particular Friday morning, David was sitting in his chair as the tardy bell rang. A female student walked in tardy and passed David on the way to her seat. Remarking to a friend three seats away, David said, "Damn, I'd love to f@&# her right here and now." The entire class heard him, erupted in laughter, and the girl was visibly embarrassed. You immediately escorted David to the door and called the school resource officer via intercom. As you held the door for David to exit the classroom, he intentionally bumped your shoulder and muttered something under his breath as he passed. You did not reply, and he kept walking, not waiting for the resource officer as you had instructed.

Repeated phone calls at 8 P.M. finally result in contact with his mother. You request a conference with her, noting in brief that you have some serious concerns about David's academic progress and future. She offers no dramatic reaction to your request for a conference and agrees to meet with you after school.

Presimulation Teacher Reflection Guide —*Angela Summers*

1. The Teacher Interaction Protocol for this clinical simulation is complex. Given that you have initiated this conference with Mrs. Summers, what type(s) of interaction(s) with Mrs. Summers do you anticipate having in this conference?

2. What goals do you have for your meeting with Mrs. Summers? Are there specific parts of David's academic performance or behavior that you intend to focus on?

3. Do you have any specific observations, notes, or statements you wish to document before this clinical simulation begins?

4. Do you have any questions, concerns, or professional issues that you wish to document before this clinical simulation begins?

Postsimulation Teacher Reflection Guide—*Angela Summers*

1. Reflecting on your conversation with Mrs. Summers, what are your initial thoughts and feelings?

2. Did the conference with Mrs. Summers occur as you had anticipated? Was it the "type" of conference that you expected?

3. Were you able to accomplish your goals? If not, what prevented you from doing so?

4. What were your strengths in this clinical simulation? Briefly describe the portion of the simulation where you exhibited this professional strength.

5. Did this clinical simulation highlight any professional skills, knowledge base(s), or dispositions on which you need to improve? If so, briefly describe the specific portion of the simulation where you struggled or were unsure of how to proceed.

6. Reflecting on your meeting with Mrs. Summers, do you have any new or different perspectives on your professional responsibilities, policies, or expectations? Were there any elements to this simulation that set it apart from the other clinical simulations in which you have participated?

7. Are there specific questions, statements, dilemmas, or situations that arose in your clinical simulation that you want to raise for discussion during the larger group debriefing process? (List below. If possible, include a time signature from the video recording of your simulation.)

Lori Danson Simulation

TEACHER INTERACTION PROTOCOL

STUDENT: BRIAN DANSON
                                  Male, 15, Upper Middle Class SES
CONFERENCE TYPE: Parent-initiated

You are a new teacher recently hired to work at Pleasantville High School, a small, suburban school within 1 hour's drive of a major metropolitan city. It is late July and you have spent most of your summer working at the school, getting your classroom established, preliminary units planned, and materials ready for the mid-August start of the school year. You have confirmed with your principal that you'll be teaching primarily 9th and 10th grade (Insert Subject) this year.

As the summer has progressed, you've gotten to know the administration, the secretaries, and support staff. In late July (15 days before the first day of school), one of the guidance counselors comes to you, informing you that a parent wants to speak to you. You are a bit surprised, as you didn't expect parent conferences prior to actually teaching any students. When you question the counselor on what this conference is all about, the only background information she can provide is that this parent (Lori Danson) and student (Brian Danson) are new to the school district and that Brian will soon be starting 9th grade. You agree to the conference and ask the counselor to arrange for the parent to come in next week.

Presimulation Teacher Reflection Guide—*Lori Danson*

1. The Teacher Interaction Protocol for this clinical simulation does not yield much information. Given that you have little data on which to build expectations, what are your goals for this parent-initiated conference with Lori Danson?

2. Do you have any specific observations, notes, or statements you wish to document before this clinical simulation begins?

3. Do you have any questions, concerns, or professional issues that you wish to document before this clinical simulation begins?

Postsimulation Teacher Reflection Guide —*Lori Danson*

1. Reflecting back on your conversation with Lori Danson, what are your initial thoughts and feelings?

2. Recognizing that you had little data prior to the conference, were you able to accomplish your goals? If not, what prevented you from doing so?

3. What were your strengths in this clinical simulation? Briefly describe the portion of the simulation where you exhibited this professional strength.

4. Did this clinical simulation highlight any professional skills, knowl-
    edge base(s), or dispositions on which you need to improve? If so,
    briefly describe the specific portion of the simulation where you
    struggled or were unsure of how to proceed. Were there aspects of
    your broader teacher preparation experience that were targeted in
    this simulation?

5. Reflecting on your meeting with Mrs. Danson, do you have any
    new or different perspectives on your professional responsibilities,
    policies, or expectations?

6. Are there specific questions, statements, dilemmas, or situations
    that arose in your clinical simulation that you want to raise for dis-
    cussion during the larger group debriefing process? (List below. If
    possible, include a time signature from the video recording of your
    simulation.)

Ashley Wilson Simulation

TEACHER INTERACTION PROTOCOL

STUDENT:	JOHN WERNER
	14 years old, 9th grade, Middle class SES, GPA: 3.2
CONFERENCE TYPE:	Parent-initiated

John Werner is one of 22 students in your 9th grade homeroom. The school schedule is a modified block schedule that incorporates a 15-minute homeroom period each Monday, Wednesday, and Friday morning. Your responsibilities as a homeroom teacher focus entirely on paperwork and logistics (long-term attendance, record keeping, collecting school fees, taking students to assemblies, etc.) You've had this group of students since the beginning of school in September, but you're only just now getting to know their names and personalities—it's hard to get to know students when you don't actually teach them anything and you see them for brief amounts of time.

Your primary responsibilities within the school are teaching 9th and 10th grade (Insert Subject Area) classes. You are now in your second semester as a novice teacher, having survived the first semester of your first year of teaching. You're proud of the generally good reputation that you've begun to establish with both students and faculty.

Checking your mailbox in the teacher workroom one afternoon, you receive a note from the school secretary, asking you to return a phone call to Ashley Wilson. The name doesn't sound familiar, but you call the cell number listed on the message slip. When you speak with Ms. Wilson, she quickly notes that she is the mother of John Werner. You recognize John's name as one on your homeroom roster. John is a small-statured, 14 year old young man. He is very skinny, has evident acne, and his speaking voice is higher pitched. He plays in the school's performance and marching bands, as evidenced by the trumpet he carries in with him each morning. He is always well behaved in your homeroom, doesn't speak much with those around him, and appears to be suffering through those classically painful teenage years.

Ms. Wilson explains that she has some concerns about John that aren't related to any subject area and that is why she decided to contact you as John's homeroom teacher. She asks if she can come in and talk with you. A bit surprised and not really sure what to say, you agree to sit down with her and arrange a time for Thursday afternoon.

Presimulation Teacher Reflection Guide —*Ashley Wilson*

1. Based on the information provided in this Teacher Interaction Protocol, what do you anticipate during your conference with John's mother, Ashley Wilson?

2. You serve as John's homeroom teacher, but do not teach him in any specific subject. What goals do you have for your meeting with Ms. Wilson?

3. Do you have any specific observations, notes, or statements you wish to document before this clinical simulation begins?

4. Do you have any questions, concerns, or professional issues that you wish to document before this clinical simulation begins?

Postsimulation Teacher Reflection Guide —*Ashley Wilson*

1. Reflecting on your conversation with Ms. Wilson, what are your initial thoughts and feelings?

2. Was this conference what you expected? In your experience, how common to K-12 schools is the issue represented in this simulation?

3. Were you able to accomplish your goals? If not, what prevented you from doing so?

4. What were your strengths in this clinical simulation? Briefly describe the portion of the simulation where you exhibited this professional strength.

5. Did this clinical simulation highlight any professional skills, knowledge base(s), or dispositions on which you need to improve? If so, briefly describe the specific portion of the simulation where you struggled or were unsure of how to proceed.

6. Reflecting on your meeting with Ms. Wilson, do you have any new or different perspectives on your professional responsibilities, policies, or expectations? Additionally, did this simulation emphasize or highlight particular school or school district policies or procedures?

7. Are there specific questions, statements, dilemmas, or situations that arose in your clinical simulation that you want to raise for discussion during the larger group debriefing process? (List below. If possible, include a time signature from the video recording of your simulation.)

David and Linda Goss Simulation

TEACHER INTERACTION PROTOCOL

STUDENT: MELISSA GOSS

16 years old, 11th grade, Middle class
SES, GPA: 3.6, Student Athlete—Tennis &
Basketball

CONFERENCE TYPE: Teacher-initiated

You are the 11th grade (Insert Subject) teacher at Smithfield High School, a small rural school with a student population of 425 students. You teach regular, honors, and AP sections of (Insert Subject). While you have several sections to prep for during your first year of teaching, you've handled the workload well, adjusting efficiently to the demands of public school teaching.

You pride yourself on maintaining high standards for all students in all of your classes, regardless of the section. During your first semester, you received a few challenges from both parents and students regarding your high expectations. You handled those inquiries and concerns professionally. You were open to parent questions and student concerns, but held to the clear and fair expectations previously outlined in your syllabi and in documents sent home to parents. Your principal has expressed support of your efforts and expectations and you weathered your first semester of teaching in strong fashion.

In this new semester, you've particularly enjoyed working with your AP (Insert Subject Area) class. Reflecting back on how you taught the class in the fall semester, you decided to implement some additional student-centered projects, where the students are much more responsible for learning the material and are not relying as much on you telling them what they need to know. In general, this group of 25 students has responded well to the different types of assignments, since realizing they would not be academically successful by just sitting idle in their seats.

As the semester has progressed, you've noticed that Melissa Goss's grades have begun to slip. In addition, she is not participating as much in class and often looks tired and distracted. You looked up her past grades and note that this quarter is the first time she's had grades in the 70s; her average is usually in the mid-90s. You do know that Melissa is a fairly matter-of-fact kid who doesn't put up with much nonsense from anyone. She is heavily involved throughout student council and is a key athlete for both the fall tennis and winter basketball women's teams. In an effort to convey to Melissa that you care and are aware of her, you have gently asked Melissa how she's doing and if everything is "o.k." She's responded to your queries in a fairly noncommittal manner, saying "I'm fine" and leaving it at that. Very recently, your AP class had a major assignment due, worth 20% of the entire semester's grade. This is an important assignment, and you checked the status of each student's assignment as he/she handed it in. Melissa was the only student who did not submit the assignment. As the final bell rang and the students were leaving, you quietly and politely asked Melissa to stay after class to speak with you. She abruptly snapped back at you, "I can't! I've got to go! I've got way too much going on to be worrying about this right now!" and stomped out into the crowded hallway.

Realizing that something is going on with Melissa, you inquire with the school's guidance counselor. The counselor checks with the other teachers, and gives you the general report that Melissa is struggling in her other classes as well. Since Melissa rudely refused to speak with you after class, you decide it's time for a conference with one of her parents. You call home and leave a message. Lisa Goss, Melissa's mother, returns your call a day later. You explain that you have concerns about Melissa's progress in your class and would appreciate a parent-teacher conference to discuss Melissa's difficulties. Lisa doesn't say much, but agrees to come in the following Thursday for a conference.

Presimulation Teacher Reflection Guide —*David & Linda Goss*

1. Based on the information provided in this Teacher Interaction Protocol, what topic(s) do you intend to focus on during your conference with Melissa's mother, Linda Goss?

2. Describe your approach to the upcoming conference with Mrs. Goss? How will you convey the data you have on Melissa's performance and behavior?

3. Do you have any specific observations, notes, or statements you wish to document before this clinical simulation begins?

4. Do you have any questions, concerns, or professional issues that you wish to document before this clinical simulation begins?

Postsimulation Teacher Reflection Guide
—*David and Linda Goss*

1. Reflecting on this simulation, what are your initial thoughts and feelings?

2. Was this conference what you expected? If not, what was unexpected?

3. Were you able to address the topic(s) you intended to discuss? If not, what prevented you from doing so?

4. What were your strengths in this clinical simulation? Briefly describe the portion of the simulation where you exhibited this professional strength.

5. Did this clinical simulation highlight any professional skills, knowledge base(s), or dispositions on which you need to improve? If so, briefly describe the specific portion of the simulation where you struggled or were unsure of how to proceed.

6. Based on your interactions in this simulation, do you have any new or different perspectives on your professional responsibilities, policies, or expectations? Did this simulation highlight any other school personnel who might assist/aide you in similar conversations?

7. Are there specific questions, statements, dilemmas, or situations that arose in your clinical simulation that you want to raise for discussion during the larger group debriefing process? (List below. If possible, include a time signature from the video recording of your simulation.)

Corinne Hammond Simulation

TEACHER INTERACTION PROTOCOL

STUDENT: BECKY HAMMOND
                                  15 years old, 10th grade, Upper Middle
                                  Class SES, GPA: 4.0, Class Rank—2nd
CONFERENCE TYPE: Parent-initiated

You are a first year teacher at Roberts High School, one of five high schools in a large, mostly suburban school district. You had a successful first semester as a first-year teacher, establishing yourself within the school and community as a fair and hardworking teacher who maintains high expectations for all students.

Your (Insert Subject Area) classes this semester are a mix of 10th grade regular and honors courses. You are the one of two (Insert Subject Area) teachers responsible for the 10th grade honors sections this semester. Your honors course roster includes some of the top sophomore students in the school and you've enjoyed getting to know them as the semester has begun. You are generally impressed with their abilities and creativity, and their eagerness has pushed you to continue to improve your own pedagogy.

In teaching this group of honors students, you believe that it is your responsibility to push them to think beyond the immediate subject matter in your course. Consequently, one of your major assignments for this 9-week grading period is a six to eight page report on a major contributor in (Insert Subject Area). You define "major contributor" as any past or present human being or significant event that has significantly contributed to (Insert Subject Area). Other than the page requirements and MLA citation format, you've intentionally left this major writing assignment fairly open, encouraging students to think broadly as they search for potential topics. As expected, some students are a little uneasy at first. Consequently, you've taken class time to check on the notes these students have taken on their chosen subjects. This has allowed you to have individual conferences with each student and closely monitor their choices of content and their progress so far.

On the day this major assignment is due, all 23 of your honors students submit their assignment, a tribute to your clear instructions and explicitly-stated late penalties for papers. You spend the next few weeks (and mainly weekends) carefully reviewing these papers, providing formative comments throughout each student's paper. When you are three pages into Becky Hammond's paper, you are angry. It is clear that she cheated on this assignment.

Becky Hammond is a strong student in your class and throughout the entire sophomore class. She prides herself on getting 99s and 100s on assignments and has made it clear to her peers that she wants to be valedictorian upon graduation. As you progress through her written report, you initially think that something is "off." As you read further, you realize that the language used consistently throughout the paper is well beyond a tenth grader's capacity, even an intelligent tenth grader. Suspicious, you take the time to type a few pages of Becky's report into the plagiarism website Turn-it-in.com. The website provides a detailed report that confirms your suspicions. Of the three pages that you submitted to the website, only four sentences were Becky's own words. Everything else was copied directly and verbatim from online encyclopedias and other online resources. Turn-it-in.com provided you with a report that is color-coded, showing you what parts of Becky's "paper" were copied from which source. You're not happy with this situation, but want to make sure that your anger doesn't influence how you address this situation. The school's policy on cheating is unfortunately ambiguous. After speaking with your mentor teacher, you decide to assign the paper a firm zero, believing that the bad grade is a fair and appropriate response to her blatant plagiarism. You note in the cover of Becky's report that she is receiving the zero as a result of plagiarism and you encourage her to see you after class to speak further about this matter.

You are watching Becky closely when you hand the class back their writing assignments at the end of the week. As students are comparing grades with one another, Becky sits quietly. You watched her when she opened the cover to her report. She looked surprised, but quickly put on an expressionless face for the rest of the class period. When the bell rang, she did not look at you as she exited your classroom. On Monday morning, you receive a handwritten note in your box from Mrs. Hammond, Becky's mother. The note is short, but references Becky's zero. Mrs. Hammond concludes the note by requesting a conference with you. You call her back using the provided phone number and agree to meet with her on Thursday afternoon. Her voice and inflection are calm and noncommittal when you arrange the time and place for the conference. You aren't surprised that Mrs. Hammond wants to talk with you about Becky's grade. You figured Becky wasn't going to accept the zero without saying anything.

Presimulation Teacher Reflection Guide —*Corinne Hammond*

1.   Based on the description of Becky Hammond and your decision on the plagiarism issue, what do you anticipate during this conference with Becky's mother, Corinne?

2.   What are your goals for this upcoming conference?

3.   Do you have any specific observations, notes, or statements you wish to document before this clinical simulation begins?

4.   Do you have any questions, concerns, or professional issues that you wish to document before this clinical simulation begins?

Postsimulation Teacher Reflection Guide —*Corinne Hammond*

1.   Reflecting on this simulation, what are your initial thoughts and feelings?

2. How did you prepare for your conversation with Mrs. Hammond? Did specific communication approaches or a reliance on evidence/data guide your preparation?

3. What were your strengths in this clinical simulation? Briefly describe the portion of the simulation where you exhibited this professional strength.

4. Did this clinical simulation highlight any professional skills, knowledge base(s), or dispositions on which you need to improve? If so, briefly describe the specific portion of the simulation where you struggled or were unsure of how to proceed.

5. Based on your interactions in this simulation, do you have any new or different perspectives on your professional responsibilities, policies, or expectations? Did this simulation highlight any school or school district policies/procedures?

6. Are there specific questions, statements, dilemmas, or situations that arose in your clinical simulation that you want to raise for discussion during the larger group debriefing process? (List below. If possible, include a time signature from the video recording of your simulation.)

Elizabeth Meyers Simulation

TEACHER INTERACTION PROTOCOL

PARAPROFESSIONAL: ELIZABETH MEYERS
        Paraprofessional for students with special needs

CONFERENCE TYPE: Teacher-initiated

You are a novice teacher who has taken a job as a classroom teacher at Smithfield Elementary. You were pleased when the district assigned you to Smithfield Elementary, as this school promotes *inclusion*, a philosophy and practice that aligns with your preservice teacher preparation. Your certification allows you to work with first to sixth grade and your principal has asked you to begin your career serving as the lead teacher in a third grade inclusive classroom.

As you prepare for the upcoming school year, you learn that you will have at least one paraprofessional working with you full-time in your classroom to help support three students with special needs. In addition, you know that a special education teacher will push into your classroom for at least 2 hours each day. You decide to arrange a "getting acquainted" conference with the paraprofessional, Elizabeth Meyers, in order to introduce yourself, talk about the classroom environment you hope to foster, and discuss the logistics of beginning the school year.

Elizabeth Meyers is working in a local preschool during the summer mornings, so when you tried to contact her, she was unavailable. Consequently, you asked the school secretary to set up a meeting between the two of you. You hear back from the secretary, and she has arranged for you and Elizabeth to meet on Thursday afternoon.

Presimulation Teacher Reflection Guide —*Elizabeth Meyers*

1. You initiated this "getting acquainted" conference with your soon-to-be colleague, Elizabeth Meyers. What goals do you have for this upcoming conference?

2. Since you and Ms. Meyers will be working together to teach and support students, are there specific topics/issues you intend to discuss with her?

3. Do you have any specific observations, notes, or statements you wish to document before this clinical simulation begins?

4. Do you have any questions, concerns, or professional issues that you wish to document before this clinical simulation begins?

Postsimulation Teacher Reflection Guide—*Elizabeth Meyers*

1. After your meeting with Ms. Meyers, what are your thoughts and feelings?

2. Were you able to address the topic(s) you hoped to discuss? Did any unexpected topics arise in conversation?

3. What were your strengths in this clinical simulation? Briefly describe the portion of the simulation where you exhibited this professional strength.

4. Did this clinical simulation highlight any professional skills, knowledge base(s), or dispositions on which you need to improve? If so, briefly describe the specific portion of the simulation where you struggled or were unsure of how to proceed.

5. Based on your interactions in this simulation, do you have any new or different perspectives on your professional responsibilities, policies, or expectations? In particular, do you have new insights on your responsibilities in a co-teaching situation, where you are the classroom teacher-of-record?

6. Are there specific questions, statements, dilemmas, or situations that arose in your clinical simulation that you want to raise for discussion during the larger group debriefing process? (List below. If possible, include a time signature from the video recording of your simulation.)

William Mills Simulation

TEACHER INTERACTION PROTOCOL

STUDENT:	MATTHEW MILLS
	15 years old, 10th grade, Lower SES,
	Caucasian, GPA: 2.6
CONFERENCE TYPE:	Teacher-initiated

You are beginning the second semester of your first year of teaching at Oak Hill High School. You took the job at Oak Hill because it was one of the first offers you received. You didn't do much homework on the school itself, but you did know that the school district is comprised of both suburban and rural populations, with the nearest major city a 45-minute drive away. As your first semester unfolded and you got to know fellow faculty and your own students, you learned that Oak Hill is known for being the most rural and "blue collar" of the schools in the surrounding area. Generally, you've found the students to be pleasant. Like any group of teenagers, there are a few that are exemplars of what not to do or how not to act, but most of the students are just good kids.

Your first semester of teaching rushed by, but you managed to begin establishing yourself as a professional, hard-working, and ethical teacher. Your have three classes this semester, but only two preps—one honors section and two regular sections of (Insert Subject Area). All three class rosters are filled to the maximum, and you carry a total student load of 90 students.

Matthew Mills is a student in your regular (Insert Subject Area) course. Although you've only known Matthew a few weeks, you get the impression that he is just "along for the ride," doing only what is barely necessary. He's failing your course with a current "40" average, due largely to his failure to turn in assignments and to perform well on in-class quizzes and the one test you've had so far. Matthew is a nice kid and is always polite when you speak to him individually. You've never had to call him down for interruptions or misbehavior. Like most other teenagers, he is chatty at the beginning of class and is quick to laugh along with his peers at a class clown who is misbehaving. He's not a leader in class, but is instead a quiet kid. You know he likes racing, cars, and anything that generally involves motor sports. You hear him talking about cars and racing go-carts all the time before and after class and he's always got a car magazine on hand.

Three weeks into the new semester, you finally sit down to enter all the grades (to date so far) into your computer's grade book program. Although you knew he wasn't doing well, Matthew's very low average catches your attention, and you decide to contact his parents to try and prevent Matthew from digging a larger academic hole for himself. You dial the phone number on record and speak with Bill Mills, Matthew's father. You request a conference with Mr. Mills, noting that you want to talk with him about Matthew's performance so far in your class. He agreed to come in and talk with you and you established a conference time for next Thursday afternoon after school.

Presimulation Teacher Reflection Guide —*William Mills*

1. The Teacher Interaction Protocol describes Matthew's poor classroom performance. Based on this information, and the fact that you initiated this conference, what do you anticipate during your discussion with his father, William Mills?

2. What goals do you have for your conversation with Mr. Mills?

3. Do you have any specific observations, notes, or statements you wish to document before this clinical simulation begins?

4. Do you have any questions, concerns, or professional issues that you wish to document before this clinical simulation begins?

Postsimulation Teacher Reflection Guide —*William Mills*

1. What are your initial thoughts and feelings, following your conversation with Mr. Mills?

2. Were the points of discussion in this conference what you anticipated? If not, what was unexpected?

3. Were you able to accomplish your goals for this conference? If not, what prevented you from doing so?

4. What were your strengths in this clinical simulation? Briefly describe the portion of the simulation where you exhibited this professional strength.

5. Did this clinical simulation highlight any professional skills, knowledge base(s), or dispositions on which you need to improve? If so, briefly describe the specific portion of the simulation where you struggled or were unsure of how to proceed.

6. Based on your interactions in this simulation, do you have any new or different perspectives on your professional responsibilities, policies, or expectations? Did this simulation highlight any other school personnel who might assist/aide you in similar conversations?

7. Are there specific questions, statements, dilemmas, or situations that arose in your clinical simulation that you want to raise for discussion during the larger group debriefing process? (List below. If possible, include a time signature from the video recording of your simulation.)

Sam Collins Simulation

TEACHER INTERACTION PROTOCOL

STUDENT:	SAM COLLINS
	Age 16, High School Junior, New Transfer
	Student, Intelligent, Jovial in Class
CONFERENCE TYPE:	Teacher-initiated

You are a first year teacher at Pleasantville High School, a secondary school in the Pleasantville School District. You are in your second semester of teaching and you are beginning to get into a reasonable pattern of teaching, grading, and keeping ahead of the discipline in your classes. Your first year of teaching—as expected—has been a challenge. You are pleasantly exhausted, though, and you recognize that despite how hard you are working, this is the right profession for you.

You are about 4 weeks into the new spring semester and you've finally gotten all of your class moving in the right direction. You teach one class of Freshman Seminar, and four classes of 11th grade (Insert Subject Area). Although *Freshman Seminar* does give you a chance to teach something new, you are glad that you have four classes of the same 11th grade (Insert Subject Area) prep. It just means that you have fewer lesson plans and modifications to make each evening as you prepare for the next day. You have begun to establish good connections with colleagues and are generally known by the faculty and staff at Pleasantville High for being supportive of students and a collegial faculty member.

Six class days ago, you received a new student in your 4th period, 11th grade (Insert Subject Area) class. You welcomed Sam Collins into class on the first day, but because your other students were finishing up presentations, it was a very busy first day and you didn't get much of a chance to talk to Sam. The next day (Sam's second day in class) was a scheduled school assembly, so Sam and the rest of the class were in the large auditorium with 400 other high school juniors. Always keeping watch over your students, you did note that during the assembly, there was more talking/noise coming from Sam's general sitting area than you usually allow.

Across the next 4 days of instruction, you've noticed that Sam has begun to get acquainted with other peers in your classroom. Sam seems to have been readily accepted and is demonstrating a very open, engaging, and somewhat dominant verbal personality. Sam does respond to your questions about the class content and gives accurate answers, reflecting a solid mastery of content and appropriate comprehension.

That said, since Sam's arrival, you've had to spend increased amounts of time diffusing minor disruptions. That side of the classroom has been really chatty, is prone to spontaneous and loud bursts of laughter in the middle of lectures, discussions, and individual work times. In short, there always seems to be some kind of verbal activity or commentary occurring on that side of the room. You've spoken directly to that side of the classroom, looking at Sam and everyone else in that general vicinity. Although nothing has occurred that has been blatantly offensive, you do believe that this side of the room is getting out of hand and needs to be reminded of expectations for behavior and on-task work ethic when in your class.

On the sixth day that Sam is in your class, you do see Sam at the center of a group of students who are huddled together in the middle of independent work time. It is clear that none of them are working on what you've assigned, and it is clear that all of these students are focused on what Sam is saying. You go over, break up the huddle, tolerate the bits of laughter as everyone returns to their work, but you return to the front of the classroom frustrated over how your normally respective group of students has gotten a bit out of hand. You've distinctly noticed some eye-rolling and flippant smirks coming from Sam, and these showed again as you broke up this student group and returned them to their work.

Sam has turned in two assignments in the first 6 days of attendance in your class. Both assignments were completed fully and received A's (a 92 and a 95). It occurs to you, though, that in the hustle of getting Sam into class in the middle of the semester, you never had the opportunity to explain to Sam your expectations for academics and behavior. Consequently, as class ends, you quietly ask Sam to come see you after school tomorrow, so you can chat for a few minutes about how the transition to Pleasantville High is going so far. Sam agrees, but gives you a skeptical look, as if to say, "What's this all about?"

Presimulation Teacher Reflection Guide —*Sam Collins*

1. The Teacher Interaction Protocol describes a new student, Sam Collins. In your first conversation of any significant length with this new student, what do you anticipate? What goals do you have for this conversation?

2. Do you have any specific observations, notes, or statements you wish to document before this clinical simulation begins?

3. Do you have any questions, concerns, or professional issues that you wish to document before this clinical simulation begins?

Postsimulation Teacher Reflection Guide —*Sam Collins*

1. What are your initial thoughts and feelings, following your conversation with Sam Collins?

2. Were the points of discussion in this conference what you anticipated? If not, what was unexpected?

3. Were you able to accomplish your goals for this conference? If not, what prevented you from doing so?

4. What were your strengths in this clinical simulation? Briefly describe the portion of the simulation where you exhibited this professional strength.

5. Did this clinical simulation highlight any professional skills, knowledge base(s), or dispositions on which you need to improve? If so, briefly describe the specific portion of the simulation where you struggled or were unsure of how to proceed.

6. Based on your interactions in this simulation, do you have any new or different perspectives on your professional responsibilities, policies, or expectations?

7. Are there specific questions, statements, dilemmas, or situations that arose in your clinical simulation that you want to raise for discussion during the larger group debriefing process? (List below. If possible, include a time signature from the video recording of your simulation.)

ABOUT THE AUTHOR

Benjamin Dotger is an associate professor of teaching and leadership in Syracuse University's School of Education. A former high school English teacher in his home state of North Carolina, he current studies the design and implementation of clinical simulations for teacher and school leader development. Dr. Dotger's work in clinical simulations has been generously supported by private and public agencies, including the Spencer Foundation, the Arthur Vining Davis Foundations, the U.S. Department of Education's Institute for Education Sciences, and the National Science Foundation.

CPSIA information can be obtained
at www.ICGtesting.com
Printed in the USA
JSHW020020160920
7960JS00001B/11